WORLDWIDE THREAT ASSESSMENT
of the
US INTELLIGENCE COMMUNITY

May 11, 2017

INTRODUCTION

Chairman Burr, Vice Chairman Warner, Members of the Committee, thank you for the invitation to offer the United States Intelligence Community's 2017 assessment of threats to US national security. My statement reflects the collective insights of the Intelligence Community's extraordinary men and women, whom I am privileged and honored to lead. We in the Intelligence Community are committed every day to provide the nuanced, multidisciplinary intelligence that policymakers, warfighters, and domestic law enforcement personnel need to protect American lives and America's interests anywhere in the world.

The order of the topics presented in this statement does not necessarily indicate the relative importance or magnitude of the threat in the view of the Intelligence Community.

Information available as of April 24, 2017 was used in the preparation of this assessment.

TABLE OF CONTENTS

Page

GLOBAL THREATS

REGIONAL THREATS

GLOBAL THREATS

CYBER THREAT

Our adversaries are becoming more adept at using cyberspace to threaten our interests and advance their own, and despite improving cyber defenses, nearly all information, communication networks, and systems will be at risk for years.

Cyber threats are already challenging public trust and confidence in global institutions, governance, and norms, while imposing costs on the US and global economies. Cyber threats also pose an increasing risk to public health, safety, and prosperity as cyber technologies are integrated with critical infrastructure in key sectors. These threats are amplified by our ongoing delegation of decisionmaking, sensing, and authentication roles to potentially vulnerable automated systems. This delegation increases the likely physical, economic, and psychological consequences of cyber attack and exploitation events when they do occur. Many countries view cyber capabilities as a viable tool for projecting their influence and will continue developing cyber capabilities. Some adversaries also remain undeterred from conducting reconnaissance, espionage, influence, and even attacks in cyberspace.

Cyber Threat Actors

Russia. Russia is a full-scope cyber actor that will remain a major threat to US Government, military, diplomatic, commercial, and critical infrastructure. Moscow has a highly advanced offensive cyber program, and in recent years, the Kremlin has assumed a more aggressive cyber posture. This aggressiveness was evident in Russia's efforts to influence the 2016 US election, and we assess that only Russia's senior-most officials could have authorized the 2016 US election-focused data thefts and disclosures, based on the scope and sensitivity of the targets. Outside the United States, Russian actors have conducted damaging and disruptive cyber attacks, including on critical infrastructure networks. In some cases, Russian intelligence actors have masqueraded as third parties, hiding behind false online personas designed to cause the victim to misattribute the source of the attack. Russia has also leveraged cyberspace to seek to influence public opinion across Europe and Eurasia. We assess that Russian cyber operations will continue to target the United States and its allies to gather intelligence, support Russian decisionmaking, conduct influence operations to support Russian military and political objectives, and prepare the cyber environment for future contingencies.

China. We assess that Beijing will continue actively targeting the US Government, its allies, and US companies for cyber espionage. Private-sector security experts continue to identify ongoing cyber activity from China, although at volumes significantly lower than before the bilateral Chinese-US cyber commitments of September 2015. Beijing has also selectively used offensive cyber operations against foreign targets that it probably believes threaten Chinese domestic stability or regime legitimacy.

Iran. Tehran continues to leverage cyber espionage, propaganda, and attacks to support its security priorities, influence events and foreign perceptions, and counter threats—including against US allies in the region. Iran has also used its cyber capabilities directly against the United States. For example, in

2013, an Iranian hacker conducted an intrusion into the industrial control system of a US dam, and in 2014, Iranian actors conducted a data deletion attack against the network of a US-based casino.

North Korea. Pyongyang has previously conducted cyber-attacks against US commercial entities—specifically, Sony Pictures Entertainment in 2014—and remains capable of launching disruptive or destructive cyber attacks to support its political objectives. Pyongyang also poses a cyber threat to US allies. South Korean officials have suggested that North Korea was probably responsible for the compromise and disclosure of data in 2014 from a South Korean nuclear plant.

Terrorists. Terrorists—to include the Islamic State of Iraq and ash-Sham (ISIS)—will also continue to use the Internet to organize, recruit, spread propaganda, raise funds, collect intelligence, inspire action by followers, and coordinate operations. Hizballah and HAMAS will continue to build on their cyber accomplishments inside and outside the Middle East. ISIS will continue to seek opportunities to target and release sensitive information about US citizens, similar to their operations in 2015 disclosing information about US military personnel, in an effort to inspire attacks.

Criminals. Criminals are also developing and using sophisticated cyber tools for a variety of purposes including theft, extortion, and facilitation of other criminal activities. "Ransomware," malware that employs deception and encryption to block users from accessing their own data, has become a particularly popular tool of extortion. In 2016, criminals employing ransomware turned their focus to the medical sector, disrupting patient care and undermining public confidence in some medical institutions.

Physical Consequences

Our adversaries are likely to seek capabilities to hold at risk US critical infrastructure as well as the broader ecosystem of connected consumer and industrial devices known as the "Internet of Things" (IoT). Security researchers continue to discover vulnerabilities in consumer products including automobiles and medical devices. If adversaries gain the ability to create significant physical effects in the United States via cyber means, they will have gained new avenues for coercion and deterrence. For example, a cyber attack on a Ukrainian power network in 2015 caused power outages for several hours.

Economic and Security Consequences

Adversaries will continue to use cyber operations to undermine US military and commercial advantage by hacking into US defense industry and commercial enterprises in pursuit of scientific, technical, and business information. Examples include theft of data on the F-35 Joint Strike Fighter, the F-22 Raptor fighter jet, and the MV-22 Osprey. In addition, adversaries often target personal accounts of government officials and their private-sector counterparts. This espionage reduces cost and accelerates the development of foreign weapon systems, enables foreign reverse-engineering and countermeasures development, and undermines US military, technological, and commercial advantage.

Psychological Consequences

The impact of cyber threats extends beyond the physical and commercial realms. Online threats—from both states and non-state actors—distort the perceptions and decisionmaking processes of the target, whether they are countries or individuals, in ways that are both obvious and insidious. Information from cyber espionage can be leaked indiscriminately or selectively to shape perceptions. Furthermore, even a technically secure Internet can serve as a platform for the delivery of manipulative content crafted by foes seeking to gain influence or foment distrust.

Global Security, Diplomacy, and Norms

We assess that as foreign countries seek to balance security, economic growth, and interoperability objectives, many will implement new laws and technical changes to monitor and control access to information within and across their borders. Some states will continue to seek to control user access through means such as restrictions on encryption and steps to reduce anonymity online. However, these states will probably not significantly erode the overall global connectivity of the Internet. Furthermore, some state information control efforts will almost certainly be challenged by a broad coalition of states and non-state cyber stakeholders, including innovative technologists, industry leaders, privacy advocates, "hackers," and others with an interest in opposing censorship or government control of cyberspace.

Although recognition is widespread that existing international law applies to states' conduct in cyberspace, how that law applies to states' use of information and communication technologies (ICT) remains a subject of significant international discussion. In addition, although efforts are ongoing to gain adherence to certain voluntary, non-binding norms of responsible state behavior in cyberspace, they have not gained universal acceptance, and efforts to promote them are increasingly polarized. Despite the existence and widespread ratification of the Budapest Convention—the treaty on cybercrime of the Council of Europe—some states have called for the drafting of new international treaties to regulate cybercrime and other cyber-related issues. Moreover, although some countries might be willing to explore limits on cyber operations against certain targets, few would likely support a ban on offensive capabilities.

EMERGING AND DISRUPTIVE TECHNOLOGIES

Strategic Outlook

Continued rapid technological progress remains central to economic prosperity and social well-being, but it is also introducing potential new threats. Artificial intelligence (AI) is advancing computational capabilities that benefit the economy, yet those advances also enable new military capabilities for our adversaries. Genome editing has the potential to cure diseases and modify human performance, which presents new ethical and security issues. The Internet of Things (IoT) is connecting billions of new devices to the Internet, but it also broadens the attack potential of cyber actors against networks and information. Semiconductors remain core to the economy and the military, yet new national security risks might arise from next-generation chips because of technology plateaus and investments by other states.

Artificial Intelligence

A surge of commercial and government research is improving AI capabilities while raising national security issues. Semi-autonomous cars, the victory of an AI-based system over the world champion in the game Go, and devices with AI-enabled personal assistants have drawn global attention to the field.

Corporations around the globe are investing in a range of AI applications including marketing, crime detection, health, and autonomous vehicles. Although the United States leads AI research globally, foreign state research in AI is growing. Foreign governments cite AI in their science and technology strategies or have planned specific efforts to enhance their AI capabilities. The implications of our adversaries' abilities to use AI are potentially profound and broad. They include an increased vulnerability to cyber attack, difficulty in ascertaining attribution, facilitation of advances in foreign weapon and intelligence systems, the risk of accidents and related liability issues, and unemployment.

Genome Editing

The development of genome-editing technologies is accelerating the rate at which we can develop new approaches to address medical, health, industrial, environmental, and agricultural challenges and revolutionize biological research. However, the fast pace of development and broad range of applications are likely to challenge governments and scientific communities alike to develop regulatory and ethical frameworks or norms to govern the responsible application of the technology.

Internet of Things

The widespread incorporation of "smart" devices into everyday objects is changing how people and machines interact with each other and the world around them, often improving efficiency, convenience, and quality of life. Their deployment has also introduced vulnerabilities into both the infrastructure that they support and on which they rely, as well as the processes they guide. Cyber actors have already used IoT devices for distributed denial-of-service (DDoS) attacks, and we assess they will continue. In the future, state and non-state actors will likely use IoT devices to support intelligence operations or domestic security or to access or attack targeted computer networks.

Next-Generation Semiconductors

Continual advancement of semiconductor technologies during the past 50 years in accordance with Moore's Law—which posits that the overall processing power of computers will double every two years— has been a key driver of the information technology revolution that underpins many US economic and security advantages. Industry experts, however, are concerned that Moore's Law might no longer apply by the mid-2020s as the fundamental limits of physics to further miniaturize transistors are reached, potentially eroding US national security advantages. Meanwhile, China is increasing its efforts to improve its domestic technological and production capabilities through mergers and acquisitions to reduce its dependence on foreign semiconductor technology, according to Western experts and business analysts.

TERRORISM

The worldwide threat from terrorism will remain geographically diverse and multifaceted—a continuing challenge for the United States, our allies, and partners who seek to counter it. Sunni violent extremists will remain the primary terrorist threat. These extremists will continue to embroil conflict zones in the Middle East, Africa, and South Asia. Some will also seek to attempt attacks outside their operating areas.

- Iran continues to be the foremost state sponsor of terrorism and, with its primary terrorism partner, Lebanese Hizballah, will pose a continuing threat to US interests and partners worldwide. The Syrian, Iraqi, and Yemeni conflicts will continue to aggravate the rising Sunni-Shia sectarian conflict, threatening regional stability.

Terrorist Threat to the United States

US-based homegrown violent extremists (HVEs) will remain the most frequent and unpredictable Sunni violent extremist threat to the US homeland. They will be spurred on by terrorist groups' public calls to carry out attacks in the West. The threat of HVE attacks will persist, and some attacks will probably occur with little or no warning. In 2016, 16 HVEs were arrested, and three died in attacks against civilian soft targets. Those detained were arrested for a variety of reasons, including attempting travel overseas for jihad and plotting attacks in the United States. In addition to the HVE threat, a small number of foreign-based Sunni violent extremist groups will also pose a threat to the US homeland and continue publishing multilingual propaganda that calls for attacks against US and Western interests in the US homeland and abroad.

Dynamic Overseas Threat Environment

The **Islamic State of Iraq and ash-Sham (ISIS)** continues to pose an active terrorist threat to the United States and its allies because of its ideological appeal, media presence, control of territory in Iraq and Syria, its branches and networks in other countries, and its proven ability to direct and inspire attacks against a wide range of targets around the world. However, territorial losses in Iraq and Syria and persistent counterterrorism operations against parts of its global network are degrading its strength and ability to exploit instability and societal discontent. ISIS is unlikely to announce that it is ending its self-declared caliphate even if it loses overt control of its de facto capitals in Mosul, Iraq and Ar Raqqah, Syria and the majority of the populated areas it once controlled in Iraq and Syria.

Outside Iraq and Syria, ISIS is seeking to foster interconnectedness among its global branches and networks, align their efforts to ISIS's strategy, and withstand counter-ISIS efforts. We assess that ISIS maintains the intent and capability to direct, enable, assist, and inspire transnational attacks. The number of foreign fighters traveling to join ISIS in Iraq and Syria will probably continue to decline as potential recruits face increasing difficulties attempting to travel there. The number of ISIS foreign fighters leaving Iraq and Syria might increase. Increasing departures would very likely prompt additional would-be fighters to look for new battlefields or return to their home countries to conduct or support external operations.

During the past 16 years, US and global counterterrorism (CT) partners have significantly reduced **al-Qa'ida's** ability to carry out large-scale, mass casualty attacks, particularly against the US homeland. However, al-Qa'ida and its affiliates remain a significant CT threat overseas as they remain focused on exploiting local and regional conflicts. In 2016, **al-Nusrah Front and al-Qa'ida in the Arabian Peninsula (AQAP)** faced CT pressure in Syria and Yemen, respectively, but have preserved the resources, manpower, safe haven, local influence, and operational capabilities to continue to pose a threat. In Somalia, **al-Shabaab** sustained a high pace of attacks in Somalia and continued to threaten the northeast and coastal areas of Kenya. Its operations elsewhere in East Africa have diminished after the deaths of many external plotters since 2015, but al-Shabaab retains the resources, manpower, influence, and operational capabilities to pose a real threat to the region, especially Kenya. In North and West Africa, **al-Qa'ida in the Lands of the Islamic Maghreb (AQIM)** escalated its attacks on Westerners in 2016 with two high-profile attacks in Burkina Faso and Cote d'Ivoire. It merged with allies in 2017 to form a new group intended to promote unity among Mali-based jihadists, extend the jihad beyond the Sahara and Sahel region, increase military action, and speed up recruitment of fighters. In Afghanistan and Pakistan, remaining members of al-Qa'ida and its regional affiliate, **al-Qa'ida in the Indian Subcontinent (AQIS)**, continued to suffer personnel losses and disruptions to safe havens in 2016 due to CT operations. However, both groups maintain the intent to conduct attacks against the United States and the West.

WEAPONS OF MASS DESTRUCTION AND PROLIFERATION

State efforts to modernize, develop, or acquire weapons of mass destruction (WMD), their delivery systems, or their underlying technologies constitute a major threat to the security of the United States, its deployed troops, and allies.   Both state and non-state actors have already demonstrated the use of chemical weapons in the Levant. Biological and chemical materials and technologies—almost always dual use—move easily in the globalized economy, as do personnel with the scientific expertise to design and use them for legitimate and illegitimate purposes. Information about the latest discoveries in the life sciences also diffuses rapidly around the globe, widening the accessibility of knowledge and tools for beneficial purposes and for potentially nefarious applications.

Russia Pressing Forward With Cruise Missile That Violates the INF Treaty

Russia has developed a ground-launched cruise missile (GLCM) that the United States has declared is in violation of the Intermediate-Range Nuclear Forces (INF) Treaty. Despite Russia's ongoing development of other Treaty-compliant missiles with intermediate ranges, Moscow probably believes that the new GLCM provides sufficient military advantages that make it worth risking the political repercussions of violating the INF Treaty. In 2013, a senior Russian administration official stated publicly that the world had changed since the INF Treaty was signed in 1987. Other Russian officials have made statements in the past complaining that the Treaty prohibits Russia, but not some of its neighbors, from developing and possessing ground-launched missiles with ranges between 500 to 5,500 kilometers.

China Modernizing its Nuclear Forces

The Chinese People's Liberation Army (PLA) has established a Rocket Force—replacing the longstanding Second Artillery Corps—and continues to modernize its nuclear missile force by adding more survivable road-mobile systems and enhancing its silo-based systems. This new generation of missiles is intended to ensure the viability of China's strategic deterrent by providing a second-strike capability. In addition, the PLA Navy continues to develop the JL-2 submarine-launched ballistic missile (SLBM) and might produce additional JIN-class nuclear-powered ballistic missile submarines. The JIN-class submarines—armed with JL-2 SLBMs—will give the PLA Navy its first long-range, sea-based nuclear capability.

Iran and JCPOA

Tehran's public statements suggest that it wants to preserve the Joint Comprehensive Plan of Action (JCPOA)—because it views the JCPOA as a means to remove sanctions while preserving some nuclear capabilities. It expects the P5+1 members to adhere to their obligations, although Iran clearly recognizes the new US Administration is concerned with the deal. Iran's implementation of the JCPOA has extended the amount of time Iran would need to produce enough fissile material for a nuclear weapon from a few months to about a year. The JCPOA has also enhanced the transparency of Iran's nuclear activities, mainly through improved access by the International Atomic Energy Agency (IAEA) and its investigative authorities under the Additional Protocol to its Comprehensive Safeguards Agreement.

Iran is pursuing capabilities to meet its nuclear energy and technology goals and to give it the capability to build missile-deliverable nuclear weapons, if it chooses to do so. Its pursuit of these goals will influence its level of adherence to the JCPOA. We do not know whether Iran will eventually decide to build nuclear weapons.

We judge that Tehran would choose ballistic missiles as its preferred method of delivering nuclear weapons, if it builds them. Iran's ballistic missiles are inherently capable of delivering WMD, and Tehran already has the largest inventory of ballistic missiles in the Middle East. Tehran's desire to deter the United States might drive it to field an intercontinental ballistic missile (ICBM). Progress on Iran's space program could shorten a pathway to an ICBM because space launch vehicles use similar technologies.

North Korea Continues To Expand WMD-Applicable Capabilities

North Korea's nuclear weapons and missile programs will continue to pose a serious threat to US interests and to the security environment in East Asia in 2017. North Korea's export of ballistic missiles and associated materials to several countries, including Iran and Syria, and its assistance to Syria's construction of a nuclear reactor, destroyed in 2007, illustrate its willingness to proliferate dangerous technologies.

North Korea has also expanded the size and sophistication of its ballistic missile forces—from close-range ballistic missiles (CRBMs) to ICBMs—and continues to conduct test launches. In 2016, North Korea conducted an unprecedented number of ballistic missile tests. Pyongyang is committed to developing a long-range, nuclear-armed missile that is capable of posing a direct threat to the United States; it has publicly displayed its road-mobile ICBMs on multiple occasions. We assess that North Korea has taken steps toward fielding an ICBM but has not flight-tested it.

We have long assessed that Pyongyang's nuclear capabilities are intended for deterrence, international prestige, and coercive diplomacy.

Chemical Weapons in Iraq and Syria

We assess the Syrian regime used the nerve agent sarin in an attack against the opposition in Khan Shaykhun on 4 April 2017 in what is probably the largest chemical weapons attack since August 2013. We continue to assess that Syria has not declared all the elements of its chemical weapons program to the Chemical Weapons Convention (CWC) and has the capability to conduct further attacks. Despite the creation of a specialized team and years of work by the Organization for the Prohibition of Chemical Weapons (OPCW) to address gaps and inconsistencies in Syria's declaration, numerous issues remain unresolved. The OPCW-UN Joint Investigative Mechanism (JIM) attributed three chlorine attacks in 2014 and 2015 to the Syrian regime.

We assess that non-state actors in the region are also using chemicals as a means of warfare. The OPCW-UN JIM concluded that ISIS used sulfur mustard in an attack in 2015. ISIS has allegedly used chemicals in attacks in Iraq and Syria, suggesting that attacks might be widespread.

SPACE AND COUNTERSPACE

Space

Global Trends. Continued global space industry expansion will further extend space-enabled capabilities and space situational awareness to nation-state, non-state, and commercial space actors in the coming years, enabled by increased availability of technology, private-sector investment, falling launch service costs, and growing international partnerships for shared production and operation. Government and commercial organizations will increasingly have access to space-derived information services such as imagery, weather, Internet, communications, and positioning, navigation, and timing (PNT) for intelligence, military, scientific, or business purposes. For instance, China aims to become a world leader in PNT as it completes its dual-use global satellite navigation system by 2020.

Military and Intelligence. Russia aims to improve intelligence collection, missile warning, and military communications systems to better support situational awareness and tactical weapons targeting. Russian plans to expand its imagery constellation and double or possibly triple the number of satellites by 2025. China intends to continue increasing its space-based military and intelligence capabilities to improve global situational awareness and support complex military operations. Many countries in the Middle East, Southeast Asia, and South America are purchasing dual-use imaging satellites to support strategic military activities, some as joint development projects.

Counterspace

Space Warfare. We assess that Russia and China perceive a need to offset any US military advantage derived from military, civil, or commercial space systems and are increasingly considering attacks against satellite systems as part of their future warfare doctrine. Both will continue to pursue a full range of anti-satellite (ASAT) weapons as a means to reduce US military effectiveness. In late 2015, China established a new service—the PLA Strategic Support Force—probably to improve oversight and command of Beijing's growing military interests in space and cyberspace. Russia and China remain committed to developing capabilities to challenge perceived adversaries in space, especially the United States, while publicly and diplomatically promoting nonweaponization of space and "no first placement" of weapons in space. Such commitment continues despite ongoing US and allied diplomatic efforts to dissuade expansion of threats to the peaceful use of space, including international engagements through the UN.

Counterspace Weapons. The global threat of electronic warfare (EW) attacks against space systems will expand in the coming years in both number and types of weapons. Development will very likely focus on jamming capabilities against dedicated military satellite communications (SATCOM), Synthetic Aperture Radar (SAR) imaging satellites, and enhanced capabilities against Global Navigation Satellite Systems (GNSS), such as the US Global Positioning System (GPS). Blending of EW and cyber-attack capabilities will likely expand in pursuit of sophisticated means to deny and degrade information networks. Chinese researchers have discussed methods to enhance robust jamming capabilities with new systems to jam commonly used frequencies. Russia intends to modernize its EW forces and field a new generation of EW weapons by 2020. Iran and North Korea are also enhancing their abilities to disrupt military communications and navigation.

Some new Russian and Chinese ASAT weapons, including destructive systems, will probably complete development in the next several years. Russian military strategists likely view counterspace weapons as an integral part of broader aerospace defense rearmament and are very likely pursuing a diverse suite of capabilities to affect satellites in all orbital regimes. Russian lawmakers have promoted military pursuit of ASAT missiles to strike low-Earth orbiting satellites, and Russia is testing such a weapon for eventual deployment. A Russian official also acknowledged development of an aircraft-launched missile capable of destroying satellites in low-Earth orbit. Ten years after China intercepted one of its own satellites in low-Earth orbit, its ground-launched ASAT missiles might be nearing operational service within the PLA. Both countries are advancing directed energy weapons technologies for the purpose of fielding ASAT systems that could blind or damage sensitive space-based optical sensors. Russia is developing an airborne laser weapon for use against US satellites. Russia and China continue to conduct sophisticated on-orbit satellite activities, such as rendezvous and proximity operations, at least some of which are likely intended to test dual-use technologies with inherent counterspace functionality. For instance, space robotic technology research for satellite servicing and debris-removal might be used to damage satellites. Such missions will pose a particular challenge in the future, complicating the US ability to characterize the space environment, decipher intent of space activity, and provide advance threat warning.

COUNTERINTELLIGENCE

The United States will face a complex global foreign intelligence threat environment in 2017. We assess that the leading state intelligence threats to US interests will continue to be Russia and China, based on their services' capabilities, intent, and broad operational scope. Other states in South Asia, the Near East, East Asia, and Latin America will pose local and regional intelligence threats to US interests. For example, Iranian and Cuban intelligence and security services continue to view the United States as a primary threat.

Penetrating the US national decisionmaking apparatus and the Intelligence Community will remain primary objectives for numerous foreign intelligence entities. Additionally, the targeting of national security information and proprietary information from US companies and research institutions involved with defense, energy, finance, dual-use technology, and other areas will remain a persistent threat to US interests.

Non-state entities, including international terrorists and transnational organized crime groups, are likely to continue to employ and improve their intelligence capabilities including by human, technical, and cyber means. As with state intelligence services, these non-state entities recruit sources and perform physical and technical surveillance to facilitate their illicit activities and avoid detection and capture.

Trusted insiders who disclose sensitive or classified US Government information without authorization will remain a significant threat in 2017 and beyond. The sophistication and availability of information technology that increases the scope and impact of unauthorized disclosures exacerbate this threat.

TRANSNATIONAL ORGANIZED CRIME

Rising US Drug Threat

The illicit drug threat the United States is intensifying, as indicated by soaring US drug deaths, foreign drug production, and drug seizures.

- Deaths from synthetic opioids—including fentanyl and its analogues—increased 73 percent in 2015 compared to 2014, and mortality from all other illicit drugs increased 36 percent for the same period, according to the US Centers for Disease Control and Prevention (CDC). Preliminary data for 2016 from some states suggest that deaths have continued to increase.

- Seizures of cocaine and methamphetamine increased along the US southwest border in 2016 over 2015.

Rising foreign drug production, the staying power of Mexican trafficking networks, and strong demand are driving the US drug threat.

- In Mexico, the dominant source of US heroin, potential heroin production doubled from 2014 to 2016, according to the US Government estimates.

- Production of cocaine reached the highest levels on record for Colombia in 2016 and for Peru and Bolivia in 2015—the last years for which estimates are available—driven in part by a decline in coca eradication efforts.

Synthetic drugs from Asia—including synthetic opioids, cannabinoids, and cathinones—pose a strong and probably growing threat and have the potential to displace some traditional drugs produced from plants. Such drugs are often traded via the Internet or—in the case of cannabinoids and cathinones— sold over the counter in products marked "not intended for human consumption." Counterfeit and substandard pharmaceutical trafficking is also on the rise, with the Internet being the primary means by which transnational criminal organizations target US citizens.

- Approximately 18-20 new illegal online pharmacy domain names are registered every day, according to estimates of the Food and Drug Administration, adding to the tens of thousands of existing illegal online pharmacies in operation.

Crime Enables Other Nefarious Actors

Transnational Organized Crime (TOC) will pose a continuing threat to the United States and its allies through close relationships with foreign states and non-state actors. Some states use TOC networks as proxies to engage in activities from which the states wish to distance themselves. TOC networks also have the ability to capture territory in states or portions of states and control it with violence and corruption of public officials. They often receive sanctuary as a result of providing social services, incorporating corruptive methods, and creating dependencies. TOC networks facilitate terrorism by providing money and services, such as selling weapons. They also engage in cyber-based theft and extortion and offer their capabilities to other cyber actors.

- Hong Kong police arrested six individuals with suspected Chinese organized crime links in connection with death threats to a lawmaker elected in September 2016 who advocated for greater autonomy from China.

- In 2015, MS-13 gang members in San Pedro Sula, Honduras provided meals to children and the elderly, shielded residents from rival criminals, meted out justice for unauthorized crimes, and halted criminals from unofficially taxing residents and small businesses. Such support to local communities undermines government legitimacy and engenders public support for the criminal groups.

Global Human Trafficking Risks Rising

The number of individuals at risk of human trafficking will almost certainly rise in 2017 because internal conflict, societal violence, and environmental crises are increasing the populations of refugees and Internally Displaced Persons (IDP). Risks of human trafficking vulnerability intensify during crisis situations when individuals often lose their support networks and sources of livelihood. In addition to crisis-induced displacement, entrenched structural factors—including political instability, government corruption, weak rule of law, soft economies, low levels of democracy, and discrimination toward women, children, and minorities—will very likely continue to increase potential victims' vulnerability to human trafficking worldwide.

Wildlife Trafficking and Illegal Fishing

Wildlife trafficking and poaching are widespread in many countries, especially those grappling with corruption, weak judiciaries, and scarce state resources. Some wildlife traffickers also move other contraband, such as drugs and weapons, at times relying on the same corrupt protectors. Awareness of wildlife crime and its impact is growing among source and demand countries, and regional leaders in Africa increasingly acknowledge the links among poaching, wildlife trafficking, instability, corruption, crime, and challenges to the rule of law.

Global fisheries face an existential threat in the decades ahead from surging worldwide demand, declining ocean health, and continued illegal, unreported, and unregulated (IUU) fishing. IUU fishing also harms legitimate fishing activities and livelihoods, jeopardizes food and economic security, benefits transnational crime, distorts markets, contributes to human trafficking, and undermines ongoing efforts to implement sustainable fisheries policies. It can also heighten tensions within and between countries and encourage piracy and frequently involves forced labor, a form of human trafficking.

ECONOMICS AND NATURAL RESOURCES

Global growth is likely to remain subdued in 2017 amid growing headwinds in China's economy and tepid growth in advanced economies. Worldwide gross domestic product (GDP) growth was virtually unchanged in 2016 from the previous year at 3.1 percent and is forecast to grow 3.5 percent in 2017, according the International Monetary Fund (IMF). Improving growth in commodity-dependent economies is likely to boost global economic activity beyond 2017. Adverse shocks, however, such as a greater slowdown in China than the IMF projects or capital outflows from emerging markets stemming from rising US interest rates, would put the modest global economic recovery at risk.

Macroeconomic Stability

The outlook for emerging markets and developing countries is improving, primarily because of stabilizing commodity prices and increased capital inflows. The IMF forecasts that growth in emerging economies will accelerate to 4.5 percent in 2017 as recoveries start to take hold in several countries. However, rising non-performing loans in China could reinforce the deceleration in Chinese economic growth, weighing on global economic and financial conditions and dampening global demand, particularly for commodities. Moreover, the prospect of higher interest rates in the United States and a strengthening dollar might lead to sustained capital outflows again from emerging markets.

Continued solid performance by the United States and increasingly stable conditions in many European states will probably help to support growth in developed economies. Many European countries and Japan, however, continue to rely on low interest rates and accommodative monetary policies to counter weak demand. Policy uncertainty also poses risks to the global economy.

Energy and Commodities

Subdued growth, particularly in the industrialized economies, had a negative impact on commodity prices in recent years, which have been particularly harmful for emerging market economies, with the exception of net commodity importers, such as China and India. A collapsing economy in Venezuela—the result of the oil-price decline and years of flawed economic policy and profligate government spending—will leave Caracas struggling to avoid default in 2017. Saudi Arabia and other Persian Gulf oil exporters, who generally have more substantial financial reserves, have nonetheless seen a sharp increase in budget deficits that have forced politically unpopular fiscal reforms such as cuts to subsidies, government spending, and government jobs. In Africa, declining oil revenues, past mismanagement, and inadequate policy responses to oil price shock have contributed to Angolan and Nigerian fiscal problems, currency strains, and deteriorating foreign exchange reserves. The World Bank forecasts that prices for most commodities, however, will increase slightly in 2017 as markets continue to rebalance, albeit at lower levels than earlier in the decade.

Sluggish growth of global demand for oil and low prices continue to discourage plans to develop new resources and expand existing projects—particularly in high-cost areas such as the Arctic, Brazilian pre-salt region, or West Africa's deepwater. Projects already under development will probably be completed during the next five years, but longer-term prospects have been slashed, potentially setting the stage for shortfalls and higher prices when demand recovers.

The Arctic

Arctic countries face an array of challenges and opportunities as diminishing sea ice increases commercial shipping prospects and possible competition over undersea resources in coming decades. In August 2016, the first large-capacity cruise ship traversed the Northwest Passage, and more such trips are planned. In September 2016, NASA measured the Arctic sea ice minimum extent at roughly 900,000 square miles less than the 1981-2010 average. Relatively low economic stakes in the past and fairly well established exclusive economic zones (EEZs) among the Arctic states have facilitated cooperation in pursuit of shared interests in the region, even as polar ice has receded and Arctic-capable technology has improved. However, as the Arctic becomes more open to shipping and commercial exploitation, we assess that risk of competition over access to sea routes and resources, including fish, will include countries traditionally active in the Arctic as well as other countries that do not border on the region but increasingly look to advance their economic interests there.

HUMAN SECURITY

Environmental Risks and Climate Change

The trend toward a warming climate is forecast to continue in 2017. The UN World Meteorological Organization (WMO) is warning that 2017 is likely to be among the hottest years on record—although slightly less warm than 2016 as the strong El Nino conditions that influenced that year have abated. The US National Oceanic and Atmospheric Administration (NOAA) and the National Aeronautics and Space Administration (NASA) reported that 2016 was the hottest year since modern measurements began in 1880. This warming is projected to fuel more intense and frequent extreme weather events that will be distributed unequally in time and geography. Countries with large populations in coastal areas are particularly vulnerable to tropical weather events and storm surges, especially in Asia and Africa.

Global air pollution is worsening as more countries experience rapid industrialization, urbanization, forest burning, and agricultural waste incineration, according to the World Health Organization (WHO). An estimated 92 percent of the world's population live in areas where WHO air quality standards are not met, according to 2014 information compiled by the WHO. People in low-income cities are most affected, with the most polluted cities located in the Middle East, Asia, and Africa. Public dissatisfaction with air quality might drive protests against authorities, such as those seen in recent years in China, India, and Iran.

Heightened tensions over shared water resources are likely in some regions. The dispute between Egypt and Ethiopia over the construction of the massive Grand Ethiopian Renaissance Dam (GERD) on the Nile is likely to intensify because Ethiopia plans to begin filling the reservoir in 2017.

Global biodiversity will likely continue to decline due to habitat loss, overexploitation, pollution, and invasive species, according to a study by a nongovernmental conservation organization, disrupting ecosystems that support life, including humans. Since 1970, vertebrate populations have declined an estimated 60 percent, according to the same study, whereas populations in freshwater systems declined more than 80 percent. The rate of species loss worldwide is estimated at 100 to 1,000 times higher than the natural background extinction rate, according to peer-reviewed scientific literature.

We assess national security implications of climate change but do not adjudicate the science of climate change. In assessing these implications, we rely on US government-coordinated scientific reports, peer-reviewed literature, and reports produced by the Intergovernmental Panel on Climate Change (IPCC), which is the leading international body responsible for assessing the science related to climate change.

Health

The Zika virus is likely to continue to affect the Western Hemisphere through 2017. Although it is causing minor or no illness for most infected people, it is producing severe birth defects in about 10 percent of babies born to mothers who were infected while pregnant and is likely causing neurological symptoms for a small number of infected adults. A separate strain of the virus will likely continue to affect Southeast Asia, where scientists believe it has circulated since the 1960s. However, scientists do not know whether the virus will cause a spike in birth defects there. Previous outbreaks in Asia and Africa might provide at least partial immunity and hinder the virus's spread in those regions.

The continued rise of antimicrobial resistance—the ability of pathogens, including viruses, fungi, and bacteria, to resist drug treatment—is likely to outpace development of new antimicrobial drugs. This resistance will result in increasingly difficult or impossible-to-cure infections of previously curable diseases. Drug-resistant forms of malaria and tuberculosis are on the rise, threatening progress in controlling these diseases. Meanwhile, some strains of gonorrhea are showing resistance to nearly all classes of antibiotics, leaving only treatments of last resort, greatly increasing the risk of incurable strains.

HIV/AIDS, malaria, and tuberculosis continue to kill millions of people annually and hinder development in many resource-constrained countries despite significant progress to alleviate the global burden of infectious diseases. Stagnating or declining funding for global health initiatives and lack of domestic resources threaten the continued progress against health threats despite the availability of more cost-effective treatments. Rapidly expanding populations, particularly in Sub-Saharan Africa, put additional stress on scarce resources. Malnutrition, weak healthcare systems, conflict, migration, poor governance, and urbanization will worsen the emergence, spread, and severity of disease outbreaks.

The emergence of a severe global public health emergency is possible in any given year and can have negative impacts on the security and stability of a nation or region. A novel or reemerging microbe that is easily transmissible between humans and is highly pathogenic remains a major threat because such an organism has the potential to spread rapidly and kill millions. Threats such as avian influenza and Middle East Respiratory Syndrome Coronavirus (MERS-CoV) have pandemic potential. The World Bank has estimated that a severe global influenza pandemic could cost the equivalent of 4.8 percent of global GDP, or more than $3 trillion, during the course of an outbreak.

Atrocities and Instability

Risk of large-scale, violent or regime-threatening instability and atrocities will remain elevated in 2017. Poor governance, weak national political institutions, economic inequality, and the rise of violent non-state actors all undermine states' abilities to project authority.

- Weak state capacity can heighten the risk for atrocities, including arbitrary arrests, extrajudicial killings, rape, and torture.

Groups that promote civil society and democratization are likely to continue to face restrictions in 2017. Freedom House reported the eleventh consecutive year of decline in "global freedom" in 2017. Middle East and North Africa had ratings as one of the worst regions in the world in 2015.

Global Displacement

In 2015, the number of people forcibly displaced reached the highest levels ever recorded by the UN. In many cases, US partners and allies were either the source of refugees and other migrants—such as Afghanistan and South Sudan—or hosted them—such as Ethiopia, Europe, Jordan, Kenya, Lebanon, Turkey, and Uganda. These countries and others will look to the United States, the UN, and other international donors to help meet unprecedented assistance demands in 2017. Ongoing conflicts will continue to displace people, keeping displacement at record highs because few people can safely return home and family members seek to join those who left. Europe and other host countries will face accommodation and integration challenges in 2017, and refugees and economic migrants will probably continue to seek to transit to Europe.

- Primary drivers of global displacement include: conflicts, such as those in Afghanistan, Somalia, South Sudan, and Syria; weak border controls, such as in Libya, which broadened a route from Africa to Europe; relatively easy and affordable access to routes and information; endemic violence, such as in parts of Burundi, Central America, Nigeria, and Pakistan; and persecution, such as in Burma and Eritrea.

- The UN estimated that 65.3 million persons had been forcibly displaced worldwide at the end of 2015, including approximately 21.3 million refugees, 40.8 million IDPs, and 3.2 million asylum seekers. Refugees displaced for five or more years are more likely to remain in their host communities than to return home, according to academic research.

- In 2016, thousands of Syrian, Somali, Sudanese, and Afghan refugees who had fled their countries in preceding years were returned to their countries of origin, which are still undergoing intense conflict. These returnees are now internally displaced in areas still in conflict.

The scale of human displacement in 2017 will continue to strain the response capacity of the international community and drive record requests for humanitarian funding. Host and transit countries will struggle to develop effective policies and manage domestic concerns of terrorists exploiting migrant flows, particularly after attacks in 2016 by foreigners in Belgium, France, Germany, and Turkey.

REGIONAL THREATS

EAST ASIA

China

China will continue to pursue an active foreign policy—especially within the Asia Pacific region—highlighted by a firm stance on competing territorial claims in the East China Sea (ECS) and South China Sea (SCS), relations with Taiwan, and its pursuit of economic engagement across East Asia. Regional tension will persist as China completes construction at its expanded outposts in the SCS despite an overwhelmingly strong ruling against it by a UN Convention on the Law of the Sea (UNCLOS) arbitral tribunal in July 2016. China will also pursue efforts aimed at fulfilling its ambitious "One Belt, One Road" initiative to expand China's economic role and outreach across Asia through infrastructure projects.

China will seek to build on its hosting of the G20 Summit in Hangzhou in September 2016, its "One-Belt, One-Road" initiative, and progress on launching the Asia Infrastructure Investment Bank to increase its global presence on international economic issues. China will increasingly be a factor in global responses to emerging problems, as illustrated by China's participation in UN peacekeeping operations, its expanding counterterrorism cooperation, and infrastructure construction in Africa and Pakistan as part of the China-Pakistan Economic Corridor.

Domestically, Chinese leaders will move cautiously on their ambitious reform agenda, maintain their anti-corruption campaign, and try to manage China's slowing economy. China's economic growth continues to be driven by unsustainable debt accumulation, but Beijing has made limited progress on reforms needed to boost economic efficiencies. Debates among Chinese leaders over policy and personnel choices will intensify before the leadership transition at the 19th Party Congress in fall 2017 when Chinese President Xi Jinping will begin his second term as the head of the Chinese Communist Party.

North Korea

North Korea's weapons of mass destruction program, public threats, defiance of the international community, confrontational military posturing, cyber activities, and potential for internal instability pose a complex and increasingly grave national security threat to the United States and its interests.

North Korea's unprecedented level of testing and displays of strategic weapons in 2016 indicate that Kim is intent on proving he has the capability to strike the US mainland with nuclear weapons. In 2016, the regime conducted two nuclear tests—including one that was claimed to be of a standardized warhead design—and an unprecedented number of missile launches, including a space launch that put a satellite into orbit. These ballistic missile tests probably shortened North Korea's pathway toward a reliable ICBM, which largely uses the same technology. Kim was also photographed beside a nuclear warhead design and missile airframes to show that North Korea has warheads small enough to fit on a missile, examining a reentry-vehicle nosecone after a simulated reentry, and overseeing launches from a submarine and from mobile launchers in the field, purportedly simulating nuclear use in warfighting scenarios. North

Korea is poised to conduct its first ICBM flight test in 2017 based on public comments that preparations to do so are almost complete and would serve as a milestone toward a more reliable threat to the US mainland. Pyongyang's enshrinement of the possession of nuclear weapons in its constitution, while repeatedly stating that nuclear weapons are the basis for its survival, suggests that Kim does not intend to negotiate them away at any price.

North Korea has long posed a credible and evolving military threat to South Korea and, to a lesser extent, Japan. North Korea possesses a substantial number of proven mobile ballistic missiles, capable of striking a variety of targets in both countries, as demonstrated in successful launches in 2016. Kim has further expanded the regime's conventional strike options in recent years, with more realistic training, artillery upgrades, and new close-range ballistic missiles that enable precision fire at ranges that can reach more US and allied targets in South Korea.

After five years in power, North Korean leader Kim Jong Un continues to defy international sanctions for his country's behavior and reinforce his authority through purges, executions, and leadership shuffles, restricting fundamental freedoms, and enforcing controls on information. He notably unveiled new ruling structures in conjunction with the first Korean Workers Party Congress in a generation, held in May 2016.

Southeast Asia

Democracy in many Southeast Asian countries will remain fragile in 2017. Elites—rather than the populace—retain a significant level of control and often shape governance reforms to benefit their individual interests rather than to promote democratic values. Corruption and cronyism continue to be rampant in the region, and the threat of ISIS and domestic terrorist groups might provide some governments with a new rationale to address not only the terrorist threat but also to curb political opposition movements, as some regional leaders did in the post-9/11 environment.

In the **Philippines**, aggressive campaigns against corruption, crime, and drugs will probably continue despite charges by Filipino critics and international organizations that it is fostering a permissive environment for extrajudicial killings. Philippine efforts to diversify Manila's foreign relations away from the United States have increased uncertainty about the future of Philippine-US security ties. **Thailand** is undergoing its most significant transition in 70 years following the death of the king. In **Burma**, the government led by the National League for Democracy (NLD) seeks to continue the country's democratic transition process, but the military, which has retained significant political and economic power and exclusive control over the security forces, sometimes undermines the civilian government's objectives. In addition, the NLD will be challenged by its lack of governing experience and provisions of the 2008 Constitution that do not align with democratic norms. Burma's Government will continued to be challenged in dealing with the status of the Muslim minority Rohingya in western Burma.

Cohesion of the Association of Southeast Asian Nations (ASEAN) on economic and security issues will continue to be challenged by differing development levels among ASEAN members, their varying economic dependencies on China, and their views of the threat of Beijing's regional ambitions and assertiveness in the SCS. Southeast Asian SCS claimants will continue to seek various ways to strengthen cooperation in the region and, in some cases, with the United States on maritime security issues.

RUSSIA AND EURASIA

Russia

In 2017, Russia is likely to be more assertive in global affairs, more unpredictable in its approach to the United States, and more authoritarian in its approach to domestic politics. Emboldened by Moscow's ability to affect battlefield dynamics in Syria and by the emergence of populist and more pro-Russian governments in Europe, President Vladimir Putin is likely to take proactive actions that advance Russia's great power status.

Putin will seek to prevent any challenges to his rule in the runup to presidential elections scheduled for 2018. Putin remains popular at home, but low turnout in the Duma elections in 2016 and sustained economic hardship will probably enhance Putin's concerns about his ability to maintain control. Putin is likely to continue to rely on repression, state control over media outlets, and harsh tactics to control the political elite and stifle public dissent.

Russia is likely to emerge from its two-year recession in 2017, but the prospects for a strong recovery are slim. Russia is likely to achieve 1.3 percent GDP growth in 2017 and 1.7 percent in 2018, according to commercial forecasts. Putin has long sought to avoid structural reforms that would weaken his control of the country and is unlikely to implement substantial reforms before the presidential elections.

We assess that Russia will continue to look to leverage its military support to the Asad regime to drive a political settlement process in Syria on its terms. Moscow has demonstrated that it can sustain a modest force at a high-operations tempo in a permissive, expeditionary setting while minimizing Russian casualties and economic costs. Moscow is also likely to use Russia's military intervention in Syria, in conjunction with efforts to capitalize on fears of a growing ISIS and extremist threat, to expand its role in the Middle East.

We assess that Moscow's strategic objectives in Ukraine—maintaining long-term influence over Kyiv and frustrating Ukraine's attempts to integrate into Western institutions—will remain unchanged in 2017. Putin is likely to maintain pressure on Kyiv through multiple channels, including through Russia's actions in eastern Ukraine, where Russia arms so-called "separatists. Moscow also seeks to undermine Ukraine's fragile economic system and divided political situation to create opportunities to rebuild and consolidate Russian influence in Ukrainian decisionmaking.

Moscow will also seek to exploit Europe's fissures and growing populist sentiment in an effort to thwart EU sanctions renewal, justify or at least obfuscate Russian actions in Ukraine and Syria, and weaken the attraction of Western integration for countries on Russia's periphery. In particular, Russia is likely to sustain or increase its propaganda campaigns. Russia is likely to continue to financially and politically support populist and extremist parties to sow discord within European states and reduce popular support for the European Union.

The Kremlin is also likely to continue to see defense modernization as a top national priority even as the cumulative effect on the economy of low oil prices, sanctions, and systemic problems serves as a drag on key military goals. Moscow is pursuing a wide range of nuclear, conventional, and asymmetric capabilities designed to achieve qualitative parity with the United States. These capabilities will give Moscow more options to counter US forces and weapons systems.

Ukraine, Belarus, and Moldova

Russia's military intervention in eastern **Ukraine** continues more than two years after the "Minsk II" agreement concluded in February 2015. Russia continues to exert military and diplomatic pressure to coerce Ukraine into implementing Moscow's interpretation of the political provisions of the agreement—among them, constitutional amendments that would effectively give Moscow a veto over Kyiv's strategic decisions. Domestic Ukrainian opposition to making political concessions to Russia—especially while fighting continues in eastern Ukraine—will limit Kyiv's willingness and ability to compromise, complicating prospects for implementing the Minsk agreement. Russia largely controls the level of violence, which it uses to exert pressure on Kyiv and the negotiating process, and fluctuating levels of violence will probably continue along the front line. The struggle of Ukraine to reform its corrupt institutions will determine whether it can remain on a European path or fall victim again to elite infighting and Russian influence.

Rising popular discontent in **Belarus** will probably complicate the government's efforts to maintain its improved relations with the United States and the EU, which are aimed at bolstering its flagging economy and preserving some diplomatic maneuvering room with Russia. Minsk will continue close security cooperation with Moscow but will probably continue to oppose the establishment of Russian military bases in Belarus.

Moldova will probably also seek to balance its relations with Russia and the West rather than pursue a major shift in either direction. The Moldovan Government will almost certainly seek to move forward on implementing Moldova's EU Association Agreement despite the election of a more pro-Russian president. Settlement talks over the breakaway region of Transnistria will continue, but any progress is likely to be limited to smaller issues.

The Caucasus and Central Asia

In **Georgia,** the ruling Georgian Dream (GD) coalition's decisive electoral victory in 2016 is likely to facilitate GD's efforts to target the former ruling United National Movement and expand political control. GD will continue to pursue greater Euro-Atlantic integration by attempting to cement ties with NATO and the EU.

Tensions between **Armenia** and **Azerbaijan** over the separatist region of Nagorno-Karabakh flared in April 2016, and both sides' unwillingness to compromise and mounting domestic pressures suggest that the potential for large-scale hostilities will remain in 2017. In **Azerbaijan**, ongoing economic difficulties are likely to challenge the regime and increase its tendency to repress dissent to maintain power while it continues to try to balance relations with Russia, Iran, and the West.

Central Asian states will continue to balance their relations among Russia, China, and the West to pursue economic and security assistance and protect their regimes' hold on power. They remain concerned about the threat of extremism to their stability, particularly in light of a reduced Coalition presence in Afghanistan. Russia and China share these concerns and are likely to use the threat of instability in Afghanistan to try to increase their involvement in Central Asian security affairs. Economic challenges stemming from official mismanagement, low commodity prices, declining trade and remittances associated with weakening economies of Russia and China, ethnic tensions, and political repression are likely to present the most significant threats to stability in these countries.

EUROPE

Key Partners

The severity of multiple crises facing Europe—irregular migration, security threats, slow economic growth, and protracted debt issues—will challenge European policy cohesion and common action. Additionally, the form and substance of the UK's exit (Brexit) from the European Union will distract European policymakers.

Migration

The EU-Turkey Statement addressing migration issues concluded in March 2016 and that tightened border controls in the Balkans will continue to limit migration to Europe. Preserving the EU-Turkey agreement, completing trade deals and making investments offered to five African countries, and ensuring the success of a repatriation deal with Afghanistan will likely remain a focus for Europe.

Security

Terrorists have taken advantage of the influx of migrants and a potential rise in returning foreign fighters from the conflicts in Iraq and Syria might compound the problem. Europe will remain vulnerable to terrorist attacks, and elements of both ISIS and al-Qa'ida are likely to continue to direct and enable plots against targets in Europe

Some European states see Russia as less of a threat to Europe than others do, even as the Baltic states and Poland begin to host multinational battalions as part of NATO's enhanced Forward Presence.

Economic/Financial Issues

The European Commission projects that euro-zone growth will be about 1.6 percent in 2017. Its projections are based on weak investment growth, uncertainty stemming from Brexit, potential disruptions to trade, and political and practical limits to expanding monetary and fiscal efforts to support growth.

Turkey

President Recep Tayyip Erdogan's narrow win in the mid-April popular referendum on expanding his powers and the ruling Justice and Development Party's (AKP's) post-coup crackdowns are increasing societal and political tension in Turkey.

Turkey's relations with the United States are strained because Ankara calculates that the United States has empowered Turkey's primary security threat—the Kurdistan Workers' Party (PKK)—by partnering with the Syrian Kurdish People's Protection Units (YPG), which Turkey alleges is aligned with the PKK. European admonition of Turkey's conduct during the referendum—including limitations European countries placed on Turkish campaigning on their soil—is further straining Turkish ties to the EU.

- Two major Turkish complaints are Washington's unwillingness to meet Turkish demands to extradite US-person Fethullah Gulen—accused by the Turkish Government of orchestrating the failed coup in July 2016—and US support to the YPG in Syria.

- In November 2016, the Turkish president indicated that he would be willing to consider joining the Russian-led Shanghai Cooperation Organization (SCO) as an alternative to the EU.

MIDDLE EAST AND NORTH AFRICA

Syria

We assess that the Syrian regime, backed by Russia and Iran, will maintain its momentum on the battlefield but that the regime and the opposition are not likely to agree on a political settlement in 2017. Damascus has committed to participate in peace talks but is unlikely to offer more than cosmetic concessions to the opposition. The opposition, although on the defensive, is able to counterattack, which will probably prevent the regime from asserting territorial control over western and southern Syria, and remains committed to President Bashar al-Asad's departure.

The Islamic State of Iraq and ash-Sham (ISIS) has lost about 45 percent of the territory it held in Syria in August 2014, but it still controls much of the eastern section of the country, including the city of Ar Raqqah. ISIS will likely have enough resources and fighters to sustain insurgency operations and plan terrorists attacks in the region and internationally.

Asad's foreign supporters—Russia, Iran, and Lebanese Hizballah—want to keep an allied regime in power and maintain their influence in Syria. Moscow's deployment of combat assets to Syria in late 2015 helped change the momentum of the conflict; Russia has provided combat aircraft, warships, artillery, arms, and ammunition. Iran provides military advice, fighters, weaponry, fuel, and Shia militants. Lebanese Hizballah provides fighters and helps control the Lebanon-Syria border.

Most opposition backers maintain their support, in part by linking Asad's regime to Iran's malign influence in the region, but their lack of unity will hamper their effectiveness.

Syrian Kurdish People's Protection Units (YPG) control much of northern Syria and have worked closely with coalition forces to seize terrain from ISIS. The YPG's goal to unite its "cantons" across northern Syria is opposed by most Syrian Arabs and by Turkey, which views these Kurdish aspirations as a threat to its security. To weaken ISIS and check the Kurds, Ankara has used Syrian opposition groups, backed by Turkish artillery, aircraft, and armored vehicles, to establish a border security zone in Syria.

The continuation of the Syrian conflict will worsen already-disastrous conditions for Syrians and regional states and maintain migration pressure on Europe. As of late March 2017, more than 4.9 million Syrians have left the country from a pre-conflict population of approximately 23 million, and an additional 6.3 million were internally displaced. ISIS's presence in Syria and ability to stage cross-border attacks will continue to jeopardize Iraq's stability.

Iraq

The Iraqi Government's primary focus through 2017 will be recapturing and stabilizing Mosul, the largest urban ISIS stronghold in Iraq, and other ISIS-held territory. The Iraqi Security Forces (ISF) and Kurdish Peshmerga with coalition support and forces of the Shia-dominated Popular Mobilization Committee (PMC) are all involved in the Mosul campaign. Faced with the eventual loss of Mosul, ISIS is preparing to regroup and continue an insurgency and terrorist campaign.

- As the Mosul campaign progresses, Baghdad faces potential tensions between the Kurds and the Iranian-backed PMC members over disputed territory while also managing the Turkish presence in northern Iraq. Baghdad has rebuked Ankara for its presence at Bashiqa and warned of potential conflict if Turkey intervenes any farther in northern Iraq. Tensions might persist well after major counter-ISIS combat operations cease as external actors continue to pursue their political and strategic goals in Iraq.

Meanwhile, the Iraqi prime minister is trying to fend off political challenges and cope with an economy weakened by the fight with ISIS and depressed oil prices. A loose "reform" coalition in the Council of Representatives (COR) exploited political divisions in fall 2016 to remove the defense and finance ministers. Political factionalism has prevented the passage of needed political reform, heightened distrust among sectarian groups, and undermined governance.

- Iraq will probably need international financial support throughout 2017, but Iraq's finances could stabilize if oil prices continue to slowly rise and Baghdad makes progress on its reform program. In 2016, Iraq's revenue from crude oil sales averaged $3.3 billion per month, less than half the monthly revenue in 2014, despite a rise in the number of barrels of oil exported. Oil sales account for about 90 percent of government revenues and make up almost 50 percent of Iraq's GDP. The United States and Iraq concluded a sovereign loan agreement in late January 2017 that could help Baghdad access international funds that it sorely needs to reconstruct areas liberated from ISIS.

Iraq will face serious challenges to its stability, political viability, and territorial integrity after control of Mosul is wrested from ISIS. More than 200,000 individuals have been displaced from Mosul due to the fighting. However, about a third have since returned to their homes, and as many as 1 million civilians might be eventually displaced, adding to the 3 million displaced persons in Iraq as of February 2016.

- Reconstruction of infrastructure and tens of thousands of civilian structures destroyed by fighting in Sunni areas once occupied by ISIS will cost billions of dollars and take years.

- Ethnosectarian reconciliation will also be an enduring challenge. Iraqi Shia, Sunnis, and Kurds increasingly view themselves as having diverging futures. ISIS will seek to exploit any Sunni discontent with Baghdad and try to regain Iraqi territory, whereas the Kurds will probably continue efforts to establish an independent state.

Iran

The Islamic Republic of Iran remains an enduring threat to US national interests because of Iranian support to anti-US terrorist groups and militants, the Asad regime, Huthi rebels in Yemen, and because of Iran's development of advanced military capabilities. Despite Supreme Leader Khamenei's conditional support for the JCPOA nuclear deal implemented in January 2016, he is highly distrustful of US intentions. Iran's leaders remain focused on thwarting US and Israeli influence and countering what they perceive as a Saudi-led effort to fuel Sunni extremism and terrorism against Iran and Shia communities throughout the region.

Iran is immersed in ongoing conflicts in Iraq, Syria, and Yemen. Iranian officials believe that engaging adversaries away from Iran's borders will help prevent instability from spilling into Iran and reduce ISIS's threat to Iran and its regional partners. Iran's involvement in these conflicts, including sending hundreds of its own forces plus arming, financing, and training thousands of Iraqi, Afghan, and Pakistani Shia fighters to support the Asad regime, has aggravated sectarianism and increased tensions with other regional states. Tehran's provision of aid to the Huthis, including unmanned aerial vehicles (UAVs), explosive boat technology, and missile support, risks expanding and intensifying the conflict in Yemen and the broader Iranian-Saudi dispute. We assess that Iran's leaders intend to leverage their ties to local actors in Iraq, Syria, and Yemen to build long-term Iranian influence in the region. Iran will also utilize its relationship with Moscow to try to expand Iranian influence and counter US pressure.

Hardliners, who believe that the West is attempting to infiltrate Iran to undermine the regime, have driven the increase of arrests of citizens since 2014 who are dual nationals. The Islamic Revolutionary Guard Corps (IRGC) will likely continue to scrutinize, arrest, and detain individuals with ties to the West, particularly dual US-Iranian and UK-Iranian citizens. This practice will weaken prospects of attracting foreign investment into Iran's economy.

Iran continues to develop a range of new military capabilities to monitor and target US and allied military assets in the region, including armed UAVs, ballistic missiles, advanced naval mines, unmanned explosive boats, submarines and advanced torpedoes, and anti-ship and land-attack cruise missiles. Iran has the largest ballistic missile force in the Middle East and can strike targets up to 2,000 kilometers from Iran's borders. Russia's delivery of the SA-20c surface-to-air missile system in 2016 provides Iran with its most advanced long-range air defense system.

IRGC Navy forces operating aggressively in the Persian Gulf and Strait of Hormuz pose a risk to the US Navy. Most IRGC interactions with US ships are professional, although US Navy operators consider approximately 10 percent to be unsafe, abnormal, or unprofessional. We assess that limited aggressive interactions will continue and are probably intended to project an image of strength and possibly to gauge US responses.

Yemen

Fighting in Yemen will almost certainly persist in 2017 despite international attempts to forge cease-fires between Huthi-aligned forces, trained by Iran, and the Yemeni Government, backed by a Saudi-led coalition. Neither the alliance between the Huthis and former Yemeni President Ali Abdallah Salih nor the government of Yemeni President Abd Rabuh Mansur Hadi has been able to achieve decisive results through military force, despite their prominent international backers. Efforts at peace talks are nascent, and both sides remain wary of the other's intentions.

As of late 2016, the fighting had displaced more than 2 million people and left 82 percent of Yemen's population in need of humanitarian aid. Temporary cease-fires have allowed for some increased access for humanitarian organizations, but relief operations are hindered by lack of security, bureaucratic constraints, and funding shortages. More than half the population is experiencing crisis or emergency levels of food insecurity.

AQAP and ISIS's branch in Yemen have exploited the conflict and the collapse of government authority to gain new recruits and allies and expand their influence. Both groups threaten Western interests in Yemen and have conducted attacks on Huthi, Yemeni Government, and Saudi-led coalition targets.

SOUTH ASIA

Afghanistan

The overall situation in Afghanistan will very likely continue to deteriorate, even if international support is sustained. Endemic state weaknesses, the government's political fragility, deficiencies of the Afghan National Security Forces (ANSF), Taliban persistence, and regional interference will remain key impediments to improvement. Kabul's political dysfunction and ineffectiveness will almost certainly be the greatest vulnerability to stability in 2017. ANSF performance will probably worsen due to a combination of Taliban operations, ANSF combat casualties, desertions, poor logistics support, and weak leadership. The ANSF will almost certainly remain heavily dependent on foreign military and financial support to sustain themselves and preclude their collapse. Although the Taliban was unsuccessful in seizing a provincial capital in 2016, it effectively navigated its second leadership transition in two years following the death of its former chief, Mansur, and is likely to make gains in 2017. The fighting will also continue to threaten US personnel, allies, and partners, particularly in Kabul and urban population centers. ISIS's Khorasan branch (ISIS-K)—which constitutes ISIS's most significant presence in South Asia—will probably remain a low-level developing threat to Afghan stability as well as to US and Western interests in the region in 2017.

Pakistan

Pakistani-based terrorist groups will present a sustained threat to US interests in the region and continue to plan and conduct attacks in India and Afghanistan. The threat to the United States and the West from Pakistani-based terrorist groups will be persistent but diffuse. Plotting against the US homeland will be conducted on a more opportunistic basis or driven by individual members within these groups.

Pakistan will probably be able to manage its internal security. Anti-Pakistan groups will probably focus more on soft targets. The groups we judge will pose the greatest threat to Pakistan's internal security include Tehrik-e Taliban Pakistan, Jamaat ul-Ahrar, al-Qa'ida in the Indian Subcontinent, ISIS-K, Laskhar-e Jhangvi, and Lashkar-e Jhangvi al-Alami. The emerging China Pakistan Economic Corridor will probably offer militants and terrorists additional targets.

Pakistan's pursuit of tactical nuclear weapons potentially lowers the threshold for their use. Early deployment during a crisis of smaller, more mobile nuclear weapons would increase the amount of time that systems would be outside the relative security of a storage site, increasing the risk that a coordinated attack by non-state actors might succeed in capturing a complete nuclear weapon.

India-Pakistan

Relations between India and Pakistan remain tense following two major terrorist attacks in 2016 by militants crossing into India from Pakistan. They might deteriorate further in 2017, especially in the event of another high-profile terrorist attack in India that New Delhi attributes to originating in or receiving assistance from Pakistan. Islamabad's failure to curb support to anti-India militants and New Delhi's growing intolerance of this policy, coupled with a perceived lack of progress in Pakistan's investigations into the January 2016 Pathankot cross-border attack, set the stage for a deterioration of bilateral relations in 2016. Increasing numbers of firefights along the Line of Control, including the use of artillery and mortars, might exacerbate the risk of unintended escalation between these nuclear-armed neighbors. Easing of heightened Indo-Pakistani tension, including negotiations to renew official dialogue, will probably hinge in 2017 on a sharp and sustained reduction of cross-border attacks by terrorist groups based in Pakistan and progress in the Pathankot investigation.

SUB-SAHARAN AFRICA

South Sudan

Clashes between Juba and the armed opposition will continue, heightening ethnic tensions and exacerbating the humanitarian crisis and famine amid a declining economy. Both sides' use of ethnic militias, hate speech, and the government's crackdown against ethnic minorities raise the risk of additional mass atrocities. The government will probably continue to restrict political freedoms and civil liberties and obstruct humanitarian assistance.

Sudan

Khartoum probably hopes to continue constructive engagement with the United States following Washington's decision in January 2017 to suspend some sanctions on Sudan. The regime will probably largely adhere to a cessation of hostilities in conflict areas—required to receive sanctions relief—but skirmishing between the Sudanese military and rebel forces is likely to result in low levels of violence and population displacement. The regime's military gains since March 2016 and divisions among armed opponents will almost certainly inhibit the insurgents' ability to make significant political or military gains.

Public dissatisfaction over a weakened economy and austerity measures, however, will test the government's ability to maintain order.

Nigeria

The Nigerian Government will confront a wide range of challenges in 2017, many of which are deeply rooted and have no "quick fix." Despite Nigeria's progress in 2016 reclaiming territory from ISIS in West Africa (ISIS-WA) and Boko Haram, both terrorist groups will remain a threat to military and civilians in northeastern Nigeria, as well as in neighboring Cameroon, Chad, and Niger. Moreover, Nigeria, with Africa's largest economy, is suffering a recession brought on by low oil prices and militant attacks on its oil infrastructure. This recession is handicapping Abuja's efforts to combat the terrorists and respond to a growing humanitarian crisis in the northeast.

Sahel

Governments in Africa's Sahel region—particularly Chad, Mali, Mauritania, and Niger—will remain at risk of internal conflict and terrorist attacks in 2017. The region's shared geography, ethnic and religious connections, and a pervasive lack of border security have facilitated a rise in extremist groups, traffickers, and antigovernment militias since the collapse of Libya in 2011 and the northern Mali uprising in 2012. Al-Qa'ida in the Lands of the Islamic Maghreb (AQIM), al-Murabitun, Ansar al-Din, and other violent extremist groups will continue attacking Western and local interests in the region.

Somalia

The Somali Government will continue to rely on international assistance, including in the areas of civilian protection, service provision, dispute resolution, security, and humanitarian relief. Progress in these areas is critical to maintain support from troop-contributing countries of the African Union Mission in Somalia (AMISOM), which plans to begin withdrawing from Somalia in 2018.

Ethiopia

Ethiopia has faced widespread public protests and ethnic tensions and will struggle to address the underlying grievances while preserving the power of the ruling party. The risk of instability is high. Addis Ababa declared a state of emergency in October 2016 and continues mass arrests, targeting opposition leaders.

Democratic Republic of the Congo

A deal between the government of the Democratic Republic of the Congo (DRC) and Congolese opposition and civil society over President Joseph Kabila's term extension has bought the regime time. Kabila named an opposition member as prime minister in April, but elections are unlikely to be held by the end of 2017 as called for under the agreement. Meanwhile, armed conflict in the east perpetrated by militia groups will exacerbate serious humanitarian challenges.

WESTERN HEMISPHERE

Mexico

The Mexican Government will focus on domestic priorities to help position the country for the presidential election in 2018 while also seeking to limit fallout from potential shifts in the bilateral relationship with the United States. Mexico will be challenged to make gains against corruption and rising crime and will continue to rely on the military to stymie criminal violence. Its $1.1 trillion economy has benefitted from strong economic fundamentals and robust exports, but changes in trade relationships might weaken the export sector and slow economic growth. Mexican migration to the United States, which has decreased in recent years, might increase if economic opportunity at home declines. Apprehensions of undocumented Mexicans fell from about 268,000 in FY 2013 to 193,000 in FY 2016, according to DHS statistics.

Central America

Insecurity, lack of economic opportunities, desire for family reunification, and views of US immigration policy are likely to remain the principal drivers of migration from the Northern Triangle countries of El Salvador, Guatemala, and Honduras to the United States. Human smuggling networks will continue to help migrants navigate travel routes and security at the US and Mexican border. Homicide rates in these countries remain high despite a decline in 2016, and gang-related violence is still prompting Central Americans to flee. DHS apprehensions along the southwest border of migrants from the Northern Triangle reached nearly 200,000 in FY 2016 but have declined sharply since February 2017.

Colombia

The Colombian Government's ability to implement its historic peace deal with the Revolutionary Armed Forces of Colombia (FARC) in 2017 will be key to the country's prospects for fully harnessing economic and investment opportunities. The peace deal ended the country's 52-year civil war with the FARC and demobilized the Western Hemisphere's largest and longest-running insurgency. Colombia was already politically stable and markedly less violent than 20 years ago. Even so, some immediate post-conflict challenges will include stemming rising drug production and addressing social and economic inequality in rural areas.

Cuba

As Cuba heads into the final year of preparations for its planned historic leadership transition in early 2018, the government's focus will be on preserving the regime's hold on power and dealing with the falling economic growth rate. Cuba blames its slowing economy on lower global commodity prices, the US embargo, and the economic crisis in Venezuela, a top trade partner and important source of political support and petroleum at generous financing terms. Havana, however, has stalled implementation of its own reform program, including changes to investment laws needed to address longstanding investor concerns and plans to unify its dual currency and exchange rate system.

Some Cuban migration to the United States via land routes through Central America and Mexico—especially by Cubans already in transit—is likely to continue despite a significant decrease following the end of the US "Wet Foot, Dry Foot" policy in January 2017. That policy allowed most undocumented Cubans who reached US soil—as opposed to being intercepted at sea—to remain in the United States and then apply for lawful permanent residency status after one year under the Cuban Adjustment Act of 1966. In FY 2016, some 42,000 Cuban migrants arrived at the US southwest border and maritime flows exceeded 7,300 migrants because of poor economic prospects in Cuba and apprehension about potential US policy shifts.

Venezuela

Venezuela's regime and the political opposition will remain at odds in 2017 as Venezuela's domestic political and economic tensions intensify. The regime is struggling to contain spiraling inflation and finance imports, creating shortages of foodstuffs and medicines in the oil-rich country. The unpopular government charges that the opposition is waging an economic war and trying to stage a political coup and will probably ratchet up repression to maintain power. Shortages of food, medicine, and basic supplies will probably continue to stoke tensions through 2017.